On This Day In

ARCATA

On the cover: Please see page 116. (Photograph by Terrence McNally/Arcata Eye.)

On This Day In

ARCATA

From the Pages of the Arcata Union and the Arcata Eye

ARCADIA
PUBLISHING

ISBN 978-0-7385-5682-6

Published by Arcadia Publishing
Charleston SC, Chicago IL, Portsmouth NH, San Francisco CA

Printed in the United States of America

Library of Congress Catalog Card Number: 2008921588

For all general information contact Arcadia Publishing at:
Telephone 843-853-2070
Fax 843-853-0044
E-mail sales@arcadiapublishing.com
For customer service and orders:
Toll-Free 1-888-313-2665

Visit us on the Internet at www.arcadiapublishing.com

The Arcata Eye
P.O. Box 451
Arcata, CA 95518
www.arcataeye.com

Dedicated to Monica Hadley,
"Party Line" columnist for the Arcata Union

ACKNOWLEDGMENTS

THERE ARE MANY PEOPLE AND INSTITUTIONS without whom the contents of this book would not have been possible: Edith Butler and Joan Berman of the Humboldt State University Library Humboldt Room/the Humboldt County Collection; Patrick O'Dell and Doe Neal, Humboldt Group; Alexandra Stillman, the Historical Sites Society of Arcata; Ashley Haubner and Lee Fuchsman, Coming Attractions Theatres; Bill Chino, CBGT, LLC; Dave White, Arcata Volunteer Fire Department; Bill Yenne, AGS Bookworks; Tiffany Frary and Erin Vosgien, Arcadia Publishing; Jon Wilcox, California Department of Fish and Game; Randy Collenberg; Ingrid Hart; Bret Harte; Austin Wiley, Monica Hadley and Rosemary Edmiston, the *Arcata Union*; Terrence McNally, Helen Wilson, Jennifer Savage and Joanne Frances, the *Arcata Eye*.

Introduction

Arcata is a small town in Humboldt County, California. Its 17,000 citizens reside at the Pacific Ocean's edge and on up into the forested mountains. They enjoy Arcata's beaches, wetlands, farms, parks, university, downtown and redwoods, all located within easy walking distance of one another.

Arcata's natural beauty clashes nicely with its burly history, a pageant of colorful personalities, dashing endeavors and triumphant accomplishments. The town's culture and politics are as diverse as its natural landscape.

For those reasons, newspapers thrive in Arcata. In any given century, there have been several swarming about, from county-wide dailies to community weeklies to niche political and music rags to zines and one-off samizdat sheets. 'Twas ever thus. As newspapers swept westward with the Gold Rush in the mid-1800s, they reached the sea in Arcata, which sprouted its own memorable originals.

The *Northern Californian* was begun in the town of Union (later renamed Arcata) by S.G. Whipple in December 1858. On Feb. 22, 1860, Editor Bret Harte published an editorial condemning perpetrators of the American Indian massacre on Gunther Island. Within weeks, he had left the county for fear of his life.

The short-lived *Casket* followed in 1860. Amid a flurry of county weeklies, the *Arcata Leader* commenced in Arcata on Aug. 2, 1879, its publisher, W.B. Thorpe, moving away after the first volume. The newspaper was revived Dec. 11, 1880, by one Austin Wiley. The well-connected former state legislator came to be involved with several area newspapers.

Wiley's four-page *Arcata Union* debuted July 31, 1886, and would chronicle the town's doings for the next 109 years. Until late in the last century, the *Union* was the central pillar in the City's information structure, its culture and identity. For its depth, relevance and sheer longevity, the *Union* is still foremost in many Arcatans' minds as the town's one true newspaper. The *Arcata Eye* still receives mail addressed to the *Union*.

The early *Unions* are a dense, enchanting jumble of folklore, formalism and funky old advertisements, lots of them intermingled with news on the front page. Gazette-style adventure serials ("Travels of a Tenderfoot") are mortared in amid folk remedies and honorable mentions. Mrs. Richard Hester of San Francisco's visit with Mr. and Mrs. Frank Graham slots in above a blurb for soothing Dikes Peroxogen Cream at Skinner-Dupree Drug Company, phone 791. Headlines are near-comic, staccato bursts of verbiage: "Should Have Good Effect" and "Goats Are Doing Well."

The newspaper was the friend of the ignored, the tool of the organized and the editor's handy megaphone. Then as now, civic movers and doers cultivated coverage and, occasionally, slammed the community weekly as unworthy. The newspaper returned the favor, trumpeting the City's prideful attainments while exposing its shortcomings as needed.

Through World War I, as the *Union* gave dispatches of Our Boys' conquests, through the Depression, World War II, the atomic and space ages and the protest era, Arcata's newspaper became more graphically interesting, always in sync with the look and feel of the time. By the mid-1990s, just after publishing its first full-color pages, after 109 years and at the crossroads of the digital era, the *Union* closed.

The *Arcata Eye* succeeded the *Union* in 1996, and the two newspapers have documented a broad swath of Arcata history. Through various twists of fate, a considerable portion of the *Union*'s archives have been scattered to distant collections. Trays of the newspaper's antique letterpress type and printing blocks even turned up under a tree in a neighborhood alley a few years after the newspaper closed.

Much of the photographic wealth remains in the Humboldt State University Library's Humboldt Room. Frustratingly, hundreds of the photographs bear no legend: fine gentlemen in wide-lapelled suits and ladies in fussy floral hats are alternately smiling and solemn at banquets, weddings, public celebrations and mysterious civic functions of unknown date.

Sometimes, as with the Spinsters' Matrimonial Club, abundant written detail accompanies the photograph. Other times, a date on the back, or a detail within the photograph offers a tantalizing and researchable clue. But many others are without provenance, dateless and disconnected from the documentation that surely exists somewhere in the *Union*'s pages.

Even though created much more recently, the *Arcata Eye*'s archives can be comparably impenetrable. Spanning the years just before and now well into digital-based newspaper assembly, *Eye* photographs dwell both in cardboard boxes and on various hard drives and other media.

That is why this book only begins to document Arcata's history. Dozens more books just like it could be created, if only one had the resources and patience to connect all the available text and image data points. But the Humboldt Room is a busy place, and in numerous ongoing research projects, that work is slowly being accomplished. Gaze into the faces of the town's pioneers, settlers and laborers and know that they walked the same streets, patronized the same shops and lived in the same homes that we do. Then look off to the side at the routine trappings of everyday life in old Arcata in wonder. Many of the same old-time Arcata buildings and family names are still with us today.

What could it have been like to attend a traveling professor's lecture at Excelsior Hall, play a role in the Society Vaudeville at Pettingill's Minor Theatre or to enjoy a True Lemon extract at Keller's Drug Store? With the sense of historical continuity the items in this book impart, it sometimes seems one could walk out one's front door and do any of those things.

In the final days of the *Arcata Union*, we used to talk about being at the end of a long parade of ink-stained scribes, photographers and pressmen going back to the 1800s. Were we to somehow all get together, one can only imagine what stories we could share and how much we would have in common. But the same is true of Greater Arcata; it has always been a town of blithe spirits and friendly ghosts. These characters inhabit our newspapers' back pages, looking back at us from across the decades and centuries, and they seem to have a lot to say if we are willing to listen.

Consider *On This Day In Arcata* an invitation to further investigate the town's newsy past, or just enjoy knowing that we in contemporary Arcata are only the latest players in its colorful, continuing history.

Kevin L. Hoover
February 20, 2008

July 31, 1886
Austin Wiley's New Newspaper

Born in Paris, Ill., in 1828, Austin Wiley served as a drummer boy in the Mexican War. His service entitled him to 160 acres of good land in his home state, but gold fever drew him westward in 1852. He arrived in Humboldt County the following year and took a job as a pressman at the *Humboldt Times* in Eureka. The newspaper moved to Union in 1854, and the following year, owner E.D. Coleman sold the newspaper to Wiley and Walter Van Dyke. Wiley bought out his partner and moved the newspaper back to Eureka in January 1858. Wiley sold the *Times* in 1860 and worked as a lumberman, farmer and merchant, repurchasing the *Times* in 1862. Elected to the state legislature in 1863, he returned to Arcata in 1866 to log and farm and, eventually, to revive the *Arcata Leader* newspaper, which folded in 1880.

The four-page *Arcata Union* debuted July 31, 1886. Wrote Wiley,

> According to a previous announcement, we take a bow this morning, and greet our patrons with the first issue of the ARCATA UNION ... As stated in the prospectus, this paper will be independent in politics ... It will be the object of the paper to aid in building up and assisting in the development of the resources of the northern part of our county.

Ten years later, Wiley stepped down as publisher, turning Arcata's newspaper over to his sons. Wrote Wiley, "In the natural course of events, younger blood must flow in the channels of enterprises controlled by those whom old age admonishes that it is time to retire from active life." (Courtesy of *History of the State of California and Biographical Record of Coast Counties, California* by Prof. J.M. Guinn, A.M.)

Austin Wiley

February 26, 1887
Firefighters Celebrate Washington's Birthday

AGAINST A BACKDROP OF EXCELSIOR HALL at Ninth and G streets, the Arcata Hook and Ladder Company gathered as part of the celebration of George Washington's birthday. Horse and ladder carts are assembled with the coach and uniformed firemen.

The annual event was described (in 1886) as "an Entertainment consisting of Instrumental Music, Drama and Song and Dance, the Dance by the 'Aborigines of Mad River.'"

The event garnered $148.25, with just $44.04 in expenses.

Planning for the 1888 version of the celebration got underway in January of that year. The *Arcata Union* reported that "the entertainment will consist of a variety of exercises, prominent among which would be dancing." The event featured the Arcata Brass Band, a small parade and a baseball game in addition to the exhibition of the apparatus.

The tradition was to continue for years. (Courtesy of the Historical Sites Society of Arcata.)

April 26, 1888
A Convergence of Odd Fellows

THE INDEPENDENT ORDER OF ODD FELLOWS of Humboldt County held a Grand Union Celebration on the 69th anniversary of its order. It cordially invited the public to join with it in making the occasion one long to be remembered and a holiday of pleasure.

Participating lodges included the Eel River Lodge, Hydesville Lodge, Humboldt Lodge, Fortuna Lodge, Anniversary Lodge, Hydesville Rebekah Deg, Centennial Rebekah Deg, Rohnerville Rebekah Deg, Empress Rebekah Deg, Mount Zion Encampment and Hydesville Encampment. On arrival of the train in Arcata, the lodges formed in line and proceeded to Excelsior Hall, where the morning exercises were held.

At 2:30 p.m., an attractive program was presented, including the Arcata Brass Band and Prof. Varney's Quintet Band, tickets 50 cents. Festivities concluded with a Grand Ball, tickets $1.50. (Courtesy of the HSU Library, Humboldt County Collection.)

April 23, 1895
Arcata Goes Electric

TWO ELECTRICITY COMPANIES LIT UP ARCATA IN 1895. The Arcata Electric Light Company and Humboldt Manufacturing Company derived power from generators belted to steam engines fired by waste sawdust and slab wood from local sawmills.

The people of Arcata were pleased with the new lights. The City Council granted permission for poles to be set up and wires strung, with seven new streetlights placed around the Plaza and on prominent downtown corners.

On June 1, 1905, the two companies merged, forming the Arcata Light and Power Company, with Brousse Brizard the president and principal owner.

In 1911, the Western States Gas and Electric Company, a Chicago firm, purchased all the lighting companies in Humboldt County. Electric lines were strung from Eureka to area communities that had been served by local plants, which were shut down.

In 1927, the Pacific Gas and Electric Company (PG&E) took over Western States' properties in Humboldt County. PG&E's representative was Arcata resident Ed Ford. (Courtesy of the Historical Sites Society of Arcata.)

September 13, 1896
A Drop to Death

LITTLE DID THE 36 PERSONS, MEN, WOMEN AND children, think when they rolled out of the Arcata Train Depot that in 25 minutes from that time the jaws of death would open in a span of the Mad River Bridge and drop the entire train of engine, tender, coach, smoker and baggage car to the riverbed, rendering the whole one mass of ruins and either killing or injuring every person on board, except three. But such was the fact.

No note of warning gave time for contemplation of the dreadful disaster that befell them; no chance was presented for escape.

The train was running at its usual slow time and had just passed from the approach to the first span of the bridge when the floor timbers gave away and the train dropped to the bottom of the riverbed, a distance of 35 feet, crushing the cars to splinters and burying the passengers in the debris.

One young man by the name of Degnan, who was only slightly hurt, ran down the river to Vance's mill, only a short distance, and gave the alarm ...

> Our Doctors all responded, and by 6 o'clock, Doctors Menefee, Horel and Hurlbut were on the ground. They worked for an hour or more preparing the injured for transport to Arcata, temporarily relieving their sufferings by the use of morphene ... gentle hands and willing hearts soon began the work of removing the injured to the various places appointed for their reception, some being carried to the Sanitorium, others to the homes of friends and relatives.

A coroner's inquest determined that the accident's cause was the breaking of the bridge's needle beams due to the decayed and unsafe condition of the timbers of said bridge. (Courtesy of the HSU Library, Humboldt County Collection.)

July 10, 1897
A Frightful Fall

FOLLOWING THE SUCCESSFUL LAUNCH ON the Arcata Plaza on July 1, the subsequent festivities of the Fourth of July in Eureka were sadly burdened by an accident that occurred in the attempted balloon ascension, turning the anticipated pleasure of witnessing the ascension into a horrible tragedy, thereby causing two men to lose their lives.

Professor Weston and his helpers had announced that on account of the wind, an ascension would be made from a sheltered point on 12th Street between the alder trees. The balloon men were on hand and proceeded with their work. Finally the balloon was inflated and the order was given to let go. Up it shot with Professor Weston on the trapeze and also with one of the helpers caught in the ropes. He rose about 25 feet when he disentangled himself and fell violently to the ground, striking on his head.

The balloon had not gone up far enough to clear the trees when the extra weight of the helper changed its course and threw it against the trees, and Professor Weston too suffered a frightful fall.

Professor Weston's real name was Charles Weston Daggett, and he was a native of Oregon. (Courtesy of the Historical Sites Society of Arcata.)

February 12, 1898
The Spinsters' Matrimonial Club

A LARGE AND APPRECIATIVE AUDIENCE GREETED the Spinsters' Matrimonial Club entertainment in Blue Lake last Saturday evening under the auspices of the Christian Endeavor Society.

All the leading society women of Arcata belong to the club. Every member was dressed in handsome and costly costumes, which some 50 years ago were in style.

The report of the Vigilance Committee was then handed to the secretary. This report gave the probable standing of marriageable young men and bachelors of the immediate neighborhood, as follows:

> Frank Douarin and Frank Knight, secured in a foreign market; Gus Perigot, quiet but steady; Todd Brizard, very active; Victor Church, firmly held; Will Dow, closely watched; Patrick Sullivan, cool and dry; Trevor Evans, riding; Charley Hansen, solid on pie, especially apple if he can't get mince; Harry Dickerson, in brisk demand; Nate Yocum, firm with good prospects of a lively movement; Theodore Hedden, ready and willing; Dave Minor, already spoken for; Ronald McMillan, first in the market; Walter Gillis, bright and happy.

After a program of several musical numbers, the members of the club decided to go to the Klondike region to find enough marriageable young men.

The mouse scare had largely subsided when the spinsters' hearts were made happy at the announcement that a man was coming to visit them, and of course everyone did her best to appear attractive. The man proved to be "Professor Makeover" (Mr. H.L. Fry), who used his wonderful "Remodelscope" machine to transform several of the spinsters.

Everyone then repaired upstairs and had a delicious lunch. The group returned to Arcata on a special train at 11 o'clock. (Courtesy of the HSU Library, Humboldt County Collection.)

July 4, 1906
The Plaza Gets a President

ABOUT FOUR DECADES AFTER ITS FOUNDING in 1858, Arcata became concerned with the impression it was giving downtown visitors, and a Plaza Improvement Committee was formed. In 1901, grazing cattle were encouraged to forage elsewhere and a bandstand was built, and flowers and benches followed.

But the Plaza's crowning glory came when, in 1905, resident George Zehndner spent $15,000 to commission a statue of President William McKinley by Armenian sculptor Haig Patigian.

The statue was created in Patigian's San Francisco foundry and survived two close calls during the April 1906 San Francisco earthquake. The statue had been knocked over, but its fall was cushioned by a plaster model. When fire broke out, it was believed lost, but it turned out that a concerned worker had hurriedly moved it to safety in a nearby machine shop. The next month, the statue was brought to Eureka by steamboat and then installed on the Arcata Plaza.

On July 4, 1906, in a ceremony attended by some 2,000 people, Zehndner presented the statue as "a gift to the City of Arcata for all time to come."

Arcata's McKinley statue is eight and a half feet tall. Its marble base weighs 25 tons. It is one of eight statues of the 25th president known to exist in the United States.

Here the statue is readied for placement on its Plaza pedestal by Severn Jacobson, left, and Brynon Smith. Charles Spaulding (wearing cap) is in the foreground. (Courtesy of the Historical Sites Society of Arcata.)

July 4, 1906
Barbecue in Redwood Park

THE DAY OPENED PLEASANTLY, WITH NO WIND and just enough high fog to keep it from becoming too warm. People commenced to arrive on trains and in rigs throughout the day, while the turnout in town was large, not many of our people leaving town.

The fire boys lined up at G and H streets at the crossing of 10th for the hose race, and at the dropping of the flag were off. The team captained by William Ericson was victorious, making the run in 40 seconds, winning the cash prize of $20.

The barbecue in Redwood Park followed. The meat had been put into the pit at 5 o'clock on the evening of the 3rd, and when it was put out at noon, it was found to be cooked to a turn.

In addition to the 1,500 pounds of meat served, there was 18 gallons of baked beans, 250 loaves of bread, and butter and pickles galore.

Marked by good order throughout the day and night, and unmarred by accident of any sort, the celebration passes into history as one of the most successful and enjoyable ever experienced in Arcata. (Courtesy of the HSU Library, Humboldt County Collection.)

July 4, 1906
Dedicating Mr. McKinley

PROMPTLY AT 10 O'CLOCK, THOSE WHO WERE TO take part in the dedication exercise gathered on the platform in front of the McKinley statue and decorated with the national colors.

President of the Day Geo. H. Burchard presented Mr. George Zehndner, who in a few well-chosen remarks formally presented the magnificent gift to the citizens of Arcata for all time to come. "I now take great pleasure in presenting it to the citizens of Arcata, and state at my request, that they never permit it to be demolished or suffer any portion of it to be defaced or erased."

City Trustee C.L. Foster then accepted the statue in the name of the citizens of Arcata and heartily thanked Mr. Zehndner for the gift. Mr. Zehndner then responded by saying that it was the happiest day of his life, and that he felt more than repaid for his expense and anxiety by having the statue made and safely placed in its present position.

Mr. Zehndner's words were received with energetic response. The life of McKinley was then touched upon, from the time when he shouldered a musket at the age of 17 years and marched to the front to do battle for the flag in response to a call from the great Lincoln. The sad tragedy of Buffalo was referred to, when, at the Pan-American Exposition, after making a speech full of broad-minded thoughts and breathing the spirit of universal good will, he was struck down by an assassin who was not worthy of being trampled underfoot by the man he struck down. (Courtesy of the Historical Sites Society of Arcata.)

JOB PRINTING
THE ARCATA UNION
FURNITUR
CARPETS
WALL PAPER

July 4, 1908
The California Barrel Company

"EXTENSIVE IMPROVEMENTS ARE NOW being made at the California Barrel Company, and still greater ones are planned for the coming year," wrote the *Arcata Union* of July 4, 1908.

These improvements, orchestrated by plant superintendent J.J. Krohn, included a new drying shed, stave cutter and wire cutters, plus more storage capacity. The plant soon went all-electric, and in 1909, a new kiln and office building were added.

Known as "Cabco," the plant was built in 1902–1903, originally as the Humboldt Cooperage Company. As demand grew, the company expanded its Arcata plant, and by 1956, when it was purchased by Roddis Plywood for more than $12 million, the company had 1,125 employees and covered 29 acres. But with pressure from the paper container industry, plus labor and supply problems, the plant was to close within two weeks of the sale, never to reopen.

This 1909 photograph shows Cabco employees on the platform of the original building. From left to right are (fourth row) John Piasco, Mr. Kimball, George Porter, Harvey Tighe, Mr. Larson, Bert McCreery, Ernest Schorling, Frank McNeil, Byron Smith, Asa Ensign, Arthur Durdan, Charley Molander, Joe Kossuth, John Dawson, George Blank, Mr. Munford, Carl Wolquist and Martin Bennick; (third row) A. Laine, Mr. Berg, Milton Samis, Frank Marohnick, Emmett Porter, Mr. Stone and Je Marohnich Sr.; (second row) Manuel Mendes, Jow Marohnich Jr. and Mr. Grater; (first row, on steps) Stacey Fisher, Chas Schmidt, Harold Welch, Chas Frederickson and Ed McClaskey. (Courtesy of the HSU Library, Humboldt County Collection.)

December 5, 1911
A Rubbish Fire Burns Blue Lake

A FIERCE FIRE SWEPT OUR SISTER TOWN OF BLUE Lake on Tuesday afternoon, completely wiping out two squares and taking the McPherson Livery Stable on an adjoining square.

Shortly before noon on Tuesday, August Brand, a merchant, built a rubbish fire in his backyard, and thinking it nearly out, locked his store and went to his lunch. The fire was not discovered until it had a good start, and it was soon evident to the inhabitants of the Lake that their town was doomed if outside help was not obtained, as they had no water pressure worth mentioning and no chemical engines.

The first buildings to be destroyed were the Brand store, the Guintolli Hotel, and the Stock and Kemp Saloon. The fire then leapt across the street and destroyed the fine two-story Odd Fellows Hall.

The net loss to the unfortunate Blue Lakers is given at $18,800, the insurance carried being $17,850. (Courtesy of the HSU Library, Humboldt County Collection.)

June 21, 1912
Mr. and Mrs. Dolson Are Wed

REV. JOHN SHURTLEFF OF EUREKA UNITED IN marriage Mr. Rush Dolson of Berkeley and Miss Atlant Roberts of Arcata. The ceremony was performed at 10 o'clock in the front parlor, which was decorated for the occasion with great bunches of huckleberry foliage, fern brakes and Oregon grape interspersed with pure white gladiolus, giving a starlike effect against the green background.

After the ceremony, the happy couple and guests gathered at the big round table in the dining room, where a substantial wedding breakfast was served. The *Union* office was remembered with a big slice of the wedding cake.

The couple were particularly fortunate in the number of their wedding gifts and silver, cut glass, linen and china were received in many and various forms. At 1 o'clock, Mr. and Mrs. Dolson left on the train for Eureka, from where they took the train at 3 o'clock for Berkeley. (Courtesy of the HSU Library, Humboldt County Collection.)

August 12, 1912
Wet Arcata's "Bubblers"

The winter and early spring of 1912 were accompanied in Arcata by heated public discussion whether the town should vote in the election of April 8 of that year to be wet or dry, to continue to allow the sale of liquor within its city limits or not.

The temperance mood sweeping the country came on the heels of the success of the women's suffrage movement the year before.

Although Fortuna and Ferndale voted dry, and Eureka, Blue Lake and Trinidad wet, Arcata split the difference and voted for regulation of the six saloons in the City, affecting their physical premises and hours of operation.

Against this background, the Arcata Women's Christian Temperance Union had for several years been raising funds to build a bubbler water fountain on the Plaza and give it to the City. By the summer of 1912, the union was ready.

James Davidson began work on the foundation across the street from the Bank of America. A series of pipes carried water to the two bubblers and also carried off surplus water from the bubblers and the dog basin, plus a conduit through which electric wires were carried.

The fountain is made from Mad River granite and is of a neat design.

Here Helen Wilson sips from the fountain Feb. 14, 2008. The dog basin and electric light have long since been removed. (Photograph by Terrence McNally/Arcata Eye.)

December 3, 1914
The First Picture Show

WHEN MERCANTILE TYCOON ISAAC MINOR became acquainted with former nickelodeon operator Mrs. Bert Pettengill, the two decided to build a theater to feature the new multi-reel feature "photo plays." "Fine New Theatre to Be Erected in Arcata," declared the *Arcata Union* in a front-page story about "Pettengill's Minor Theatre."

Ground was broken at 10th and H streets April 2, 1914, and on Thursday, December 3 of that year, the theater was dedicated with music, speeches and two showings of what the *Union* called "an exciting photo play in five acts," a silent film titled *The Chimes*, by Charles Dickens.

The evening's festivities began with "special music" composed for the occasion, a piece titled "Greetings March, the Minor," performed by a five-piece orchestra. This was followed by "well chosen remarks" by Geo. H. Burchard, who then introduced Minor.

Mindful of the San Francisco earthquake and fire six years previous, Minor extolled the 524-seat, $20,000 edifice's "safety first" features, including 13-inch concrete walls, numerous exits and a fireproof roof. Minor "humorously stated that if the whole town should burn down, he could shut himself up in the theatre and feel perfectly safe." Pettengill then spoke, saying she felt she had been formally introduced to each audience member and hoped to often see them at the theater.

The stage curtain was then raised, and, bathed in colored lights, a gondola bearing three little girls in white moved to center stage. Two more girls bearing golden harps stood at either end of the gondola as Doris Mellinger broke a large bottle of perfumery and intoned, "I christen thee Pettengill's Minor Theatre." Eight pigeons were then released from the stage to the fanfare of the orchestra. (Courtesy of the HSU Library, Humboldt County Collection.)

March 11, 1915
Our Beautiful Plaza

A. JOHANSEN, PROPRIETOR OF THE EEL RIVER Nursery, located near Fortuna, has been in Arcata for a couple of days this week setting out a large number of beautiful plants and shrubs to the Plaza. This improvement was arranged for a number of months ago, the expense being borne jointly by the Woman's Club of Arcata and the city fathers, Mrs. A. Brizard being the Chairman of the Woman's Club Committee.

Some time ago, eight diamond-shaped plots were prepared at the four corners of the Plaza and made ready for planting, the plants and shrubs having been selected some time in advance.

At the request of the editor, Mr. Johansen handed in a list of the botanical names of the different plants recently set out, and while our typewriter broke down trying to spell some of them, we are glad we will not be called upon to pronounce them. The list looks something like a Russian war map.

There is no doubt that if all these plants live up to their literary reputations, our Plaza will be made more beautiful as time goes on, and while our people will probably not be able to call them by their first names for some time to come, we hope everybody, especially the stray dogs, will treat our botanical arrivals from Fortuna with due kindness and consideration.

Here the Plaza receives a rare blanket of white remembered as the Snow of 1915. (Courtesy of the HSU Library, Humboldt County Collection.)

April 26, 1915
Arcata's Beautiful New Hotel

THE NEW HOTEL ARCATA STANDS ON THE corner of Ninth and G streets, facing our pretty little Plaza, diagonally across the street from the *Union* office.

It is of solid brick construction with 13-inch walls. The entrance to the $80,000 hotel is most attractive and through an open vestibule 12 feet wide and seven feet deep, and tiled floor. A base of Verdi marble 18 inches deep runs around the inside of the vestibule walls, above which is handsome white Alaskan marble finished with a high polish.

Entering the hotel lobby through heavy oak and plate glass doors, swinging both directions, the traveler steps into a passageway 13 feet wide between two pillars, and running back 48 feet.

On Monday, April 26th, the new hotel was thrown open for both "eats" and "sleeps." Mrs. A. Huemann, and daughter Miss Helene, were on hand to receive the lady visitors. Boyer's five-piece orchestra played sweet music, and soon the lobbies and rooms were filled with members of either sex.

The Hotel Arcata will be run on the European plan, and while meals will be served a la carte, it will be possible to arrange for board and room by the week or month. Every effort will be made to advertise the house through the excellence of the cuisine, and the reasonable prices charged.

While some great general has remarked that "an army travels upon its belly," the reputation of a successful hotel rests upon its kitchen. A 35 cent lunch and dinner for the same price will be served daily, and a cup of coffee can be secured for breakfast if necessary, the intention being to make the dining room a popular eating place, for the public generally, not being confined entirely to those stopping at the hotel.

The Hotel Arcata is pictured in 2008, as viewed from the Arcata Union building. (Photograph by Terrence McNally/Arcata Eye.)

January 13, 1917
The Stranding of the USS Milwaukee

ORIGINALLY NAMED GARFISH, USS H-3, A 358-ton H-1 class submarine was launched in July 1913 for duty along the U.S. Pacific coast. Demanding weather in the region caught up with the H-3 when it became stranded on Samoa Beach, near Arcata, in mid-December 1916.

Brought in to tow out the H-3 was the USS Milwaukee, a 9,700-ton St. Louis class protected cruiser. On Jan. 12, 1917, after many failed attempts and the loss of a sailor's life, a heavy steel towing cable was connected from the H-3's bow to the stern of the cruiser, which was anchored several hundred yards offshore outside the surf zone.

In the fog and darkness, one of two restraining lines running from the monitor Cheyenne to the Milwaukee's starboard bow parted. Currents pushed the cruiser southward, and attending tug Iriquois, outmatched, cut itself free of the other restraining line.

The Milwaukee's crew tried to cut the steel cable between its stern and the H-3, but it was too heavy for the hacksaws. It bound the cruiser to the marooned submarine, and the current and waves drove the Milwaukee inexorably into the shore.

Its 21,000-horsepower engines were helpless against the sideways force of the current and the cable's backward pull. Anchors dropped into shallow water were useless. By 4 a.m. on January 13, the Milwaukee was hard aground, broadside to the beach. Pounding surf rolled its hull, which let in the sea, extinguishing the ship's boilers. The Milwaukee was beyond saving, and its endangered crew, some 450 men, was rescued with no lives lost.

Survivors were sent by train to the Mare Island Navy Yard within days, while others remained behind to begin salvage. The USS Milwaukee was formally decommissioned in early March 1917. Its hull, stripped by salvers and broken in two by the power of the Pacific coast surf, was sold in August 1919. (Courtesy of the HSU Library, Humboldt County Collection.)

June 26, 1919
Dry Arcata

ON MONDAY, JUNE 30, SIX PLACES AROUND the square in Arcata will cease to exist as licensed saloons. On Tuesday, July 1, the wartime Prohibition laws will go into effect, and the open bar, an institution since the pioneer days of California, will cease to operate.

In making a hasty canvas of the situation, it is learned that only one or perhaps two of the places will be vacated by their tenants on July 1.

C.B. Nixon, of the White Front saloon on 9th Street, will conduct his place as a pool room and soft drink house, having two billiard and pool tables. The Huck & Walsh saloon on the corner of 9th and H streets will continue as a soft drink place.

The six saloons in Arcata have been paying into the City treasury yearly the sum of $2,520, or $420 a year apiece. The City trustees at their next meeting will meet the changed financial condition probably by raising the amounts paid in for business licenses and increasing the list of businesses, and also by raising the property assessment.

The matter of providing a center which will in a measure take the place of the open saloon is another problem that the town must face. Already the City authorities, heads of industries employing men, and other organizations, have informally discussed this important matter. (Courtesy of the HSU Library, Humboldt County Collection.)

September 25, 1919
The Arcata Fair

EXCELSIOR HALL IS BEING TRANSFORMED INTO an emporium of exhibits for the Northern Humboldt Fair, held in Arcata for three days in September.

Exhibit classes include fine arts, domestic arts, industries, potatoes and vegetables and junior industries.

Exhibitors are advised to "make a loud noise." Frames of pictures should be "rubbed up." All preserved and canned goods must be shown in lots of three, except pickles and sauces, shown in "one of a kind," unless the exhibitor prefers two or more of a kind.

All exhibits in Department 2, except bread, should be brought in on the plate or dish on which it is to be shown. Goods in glasses or in glass jars must not have names of owners, but have paper with identification marks in envelopes, which must be pinned to the entry and which will be taken care of by the Manager. Every glass or jar should have the name of contents on a neat label such as "Bartlett Pears," etc.

Exhibitors are advised to make application at once for stalls for cattle, coops for chickens, or hutches for rabbits. (Courtesy of the HSU Library, Humboldt County Collection.)

February 23, 1922
Humboldt State Teachers College

THE 1920S ROARED FOR HUMBOLDT STATE Teachers College, beginning with the installation of the campus's first permanent building atop Preston Ridge. It was called the Main Building or Administration Building until renamed Founders Hall in 1959.

The building housed classrooms, faculty and administrative offices, a library and an auditorium. The east wing housed a training school for elementary teachers. Thirty-nine arches and doorways remained open air until 1927.

The Feb. 23, 1922, *Arcata Union* extolled the new building:

> At the north end of each floor is a demonstration room, for the purpose of showing prospective teachers the most perfect kind of teaching that can be done, which is a new and advanced idea in teacher training ...
>
> Ordinarily class rooms are assigned for teacher uses to conduct recitations in and as a sitting room in vacant periods. The class rooms at Humboldt State Teachers College cost $18,000, which makes them too expensive to use as sitting rooms. Therefore, offices have been provided for faculty members to be used during periods when the instructors are not conducting recitations.

(Courtesy of the HSU Library, Humboldt County Collection.)

January 3, 1929
Seely & Titlow
Progressive Pioneers

MODERN EFFICIENCIES ABOUND AT THE SEELY & Titlow merchandising firm at 10th and I streets. The progressive pioneer Arcata merchandising firm has recently completed a new building and remodeled a portion of its present edifice.

Special rooms hold perishables; a large mezzanine floor is served by a freight elevator, with increased efficiency the result. By utilizing the former warehouse and removing a partition, a building 70 by 115 feet has been built to harmonize with the adjacent building and neatly painted in light, attractive shades, suitably trimmed.

The difficulty of keeping rats and mice from the flour stock has been overcome by the use of a room 15 by 20 feet on the east side of the warehouse. This room is absolutely rodent proof, made so by the use of metal lining and heavy galvanized wire of small mesh.

Adjoining this room is a potato storage room, 12 by 15 feet, also rodent proof, where several tons of potatoes can be stored for the retail trade. This room is kept dark, which is best for potatoes, and an electric switch at the door illuminates the place when necessary to remove stock.

Here at left is seen the dry goods shop, included in the Seely & Titlow store at 10th and I streets, offering a wide variety of items ranging from canned foods and clothing to seeds and laundry soap. Tracked ladders aid in obtaining items from tall shelves. (Courtesy of the Historical Sites Society of Arcata.)

March 28, 1929
High Class Entertainment

A NEW ATTENDANCE RECORD WAS SET BY the Humboldt Collegians when they played to 1,675 persons in two days at the Minor Theatre last Friday and Saturday. Two hours of high class entertainment sent the audience away smiling.

Every number on the program was enthusiastically received and much credit being due Carl Bowman, director of dramatics and public speaking, and Esther Sather, director of music at the college, for their splendid work in training the players.

Manager H.R. Poultney has had a busy time and his successful work is evidenced by the large audiences that have so far greeted the players.

It would be difficult to select any outstanding number on the program, as all of the young entertainers were deserving of special mention.

The stage settings and tasteful costuming showed that no detail was overlooked. Herbert Inskip as accompanist of all the musical numbers was kept busy and his piano recitals were highly enjoyed. The tumbling act of Ione and Ronald Russel (brother and sister) was a new novelty that made a hit with the audience.

Here Minor Theatre Assistant Manager Ashley Haubner offers a tour of the original dressing rooms below the Minor Theatre's stage on Feb. 13, 2008. Inside the tiny cubicles, painters have spared actors' graffiti dated 1929. (Photograph by Kevin L. Hoover/Arcata Eye.)

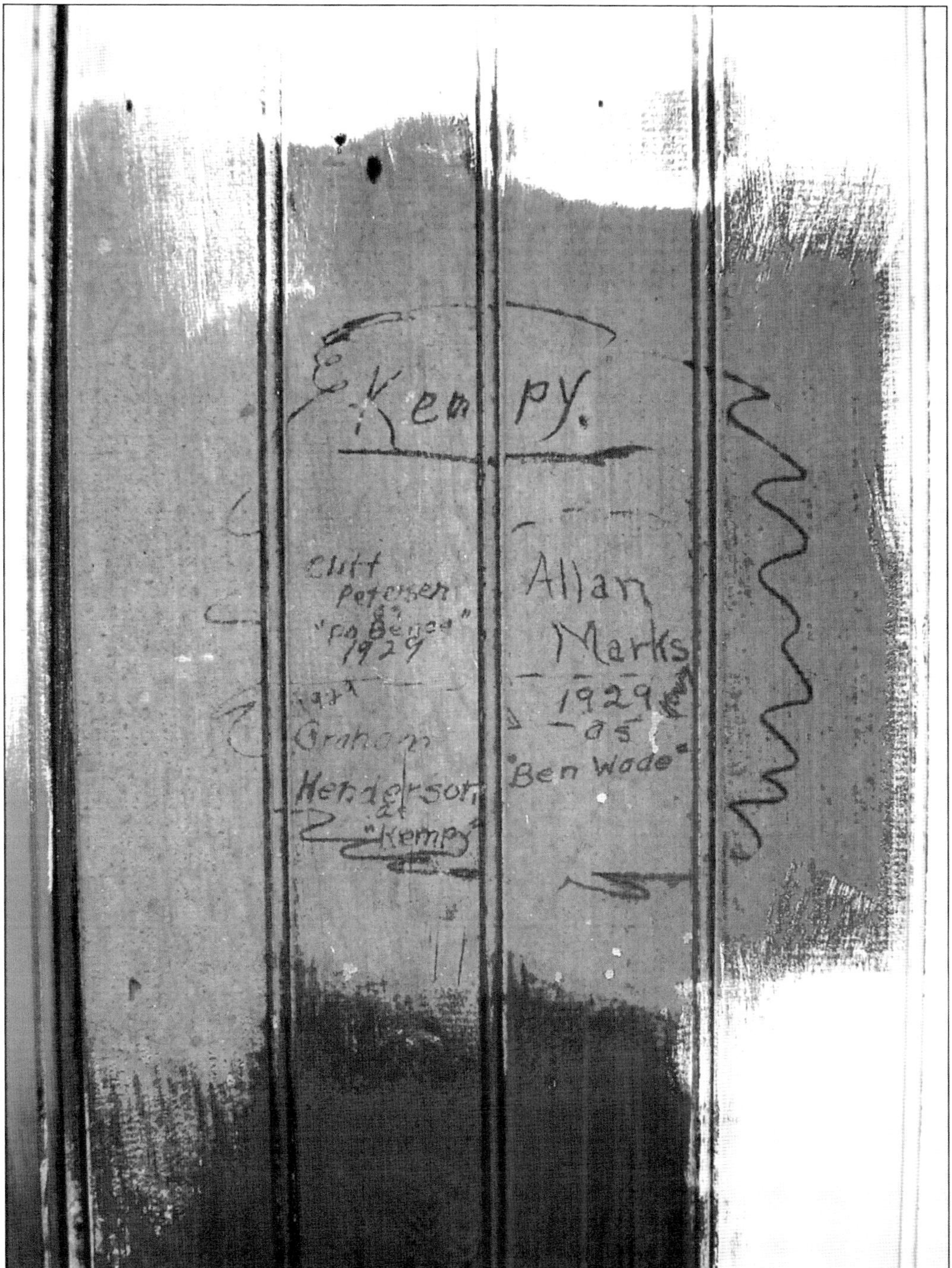
Kempy.
Petersen
1929
Allan
Marks
1929
"Ben Wade"
Henderson
"Kempy"

November 16, 1934
Arcata's Champions

AT THE REGULAR MEETING OF THE ARCATA High School Trustees held Monday, the matter of properly rewarding the members of the 1935 championship high school football team was brought before the board by Principal Cooperrider. The Trustees authorized purchase of souvenir gold footballs and Chenille tiger emblems for sweaters for Coach William McKittrick's protégés, of which the entire community are proud.

The following boys will receive gold footballs: Frank Simas, fullback; Harry Wineroth, quarterback; Frank Ricci, halfback; Joe Ramos, halfback; Keith Emmenegger, halfback; Ray Grand, center; Rube Mason, guard; O.V. Adkins, guard; Richard Jarboe, tackle; Willard Dearing, tackle; Frank Costa, end; Tony Oliveira, end; Otho Davis, center and end; Amelio Macinata, guard and tackle; Lee Seidell, end and quarterback; Carl Nielsen, guard and tackle; Edward, end; Charles Taylor, tackle.

The following players were out for practice for the entire season and though they did not get into any of the league games, did their best, and were rewarded with Chenille emblems in the form of a tiger head with the word "Arcata" above and a football suspended below with the word "Champs" lettered on it. They are an especially attractive emblem.

Emblem winners are Quentin Sawyer, James Dwiggins, Herbert Carlson, Axil Lindgren, Ned Barsuglia, Robert Morrison, Dan Grace, Clyde Johnson, Charley Macinata, Casper Torp, Martin Cabalzar, Laverne Elmore, Charley Hunt. (Courtesy of the HSU Library, Humboldt County Collection.)

September 9, 1935
The Pioneer Luncheon

PIONEERS WHO LIVED IN THIS CITY IN 1863 WERE honored at an elaborate banquet held Monday noon at the Hotel Arcata by Brizard's. Pictures of the group were taken before the dinner and acquaintances renewed. The dinner was served on prettily appointed tables arranged in a square.

Nearly 50 people were served a delicious banquet, with saleswomen of the Brizard Company assisting in the servings. Most of those present were dressed in the garb in vogue in 1863, and recollections of old times were told by pioneer speakers. Henry Brizard was toastmaster and introduced the guests and rendered everyone a most cordial greeting.

Will N. Spangle sang "The End of a Perfect Day" to conclude the affair. (Courtesy of the HSU Library, Humboldt County Collection.)

March 25, 1943
Trinity Hospital Reborn

FIFTEEN PATIENTS, TWO NEWBORN BABIES AND staff were on hand the night of Feb. 3, 1943, when a fire broke out in a broom closet at historic Trinity Hospital.

Created from the former family home of Dr. George McKinnon, the hospital was operated by the Sisters of St. Joseph of Orange from 1927 through the Great Depression and right up until the night of the fire.

Discovered at 2:05 a.m., the fire forced evacuation of the hospital. Mrs. Arnold Nielsen's baby, born just an hour earlier, was carried outside by Annette Johnson, night supervising nurse. Laurel Wood of Crannell dropped her six-day-old son to waiting rescuers from her second-story window, then leapt to safety herself.

Despite serious burns, building superintendent Gunnar Lagefoged stayed at the scene to fight the flames before seeking medical treatment for himself.

Reconstruction began the following month, with a full city block at 14th and C streets purchased by the Arcata Chamber of Commerce. The Chamber and Arcata Volunteer Fire Department jointly staged a benefit dance to help fund the new Trinity Hospital. Trinity Hospital is pictured here in 2008. Presently between owners, the hospital is vacant and has become somewhat overgrown. (Photograph by Terrence McNally/ Arcata Eye.)

January 19, 1951
Open House at the New Post Office

THE ARCATA POST OFFICE DEDICATION AND open house honored Paul A. Brizard, founder of Brizard Store. Postal inspector Don Lambert of San Francisco delivered the main address.

The open house featured public inspection of all the postal facilities, with the local post office staff on hand to demonstrate the new equipment and the methods of handling Arcata's city and rural mail.

Brizard was, in earlier days, in charge of the pack trains between Arcata, Blue Lake and Hoopa. Brizard also holds the honor of delivering the first parcel post between Sawyer's Bar and Hoopa.

"We are very proud to have had a part in the construction and location of this new asset to our community life, the new Post Office on the Plaza," said Brizard. "We have always been actively interested in the community and in helping the betterment of the area."

Prior to the open house and honor ceremonies for Brizard, the Arcata Chamber of Commerce held an informal luncheon and get-together honoring the postal officials at the Big Four restaurant. (Courtesy of the HSU Library, Humboldt County Collection.)

REDWOOD
KIEM

August 9, 1963
Gaieties at the Minor

After renovating the Minor Theatre, the Union Town Players launched the first of three summer repertory seasons in 1961. The first season featured *Picnic*, *Only an Orphan Girl* and *Arsenic and Old Lace*.

Offerings in 1962 included *Auntie Mame*, *Come Back Little Sheba* and *Union Town Gaities*. The 1963 repertory featured *Harvey*, *The Children's Hour* and *The Boy Friend*.

After three successful seasons, the Union Town Players disbanded. Participants were teachers and professionals who had devoted their vacations to producing the plays. In its final season, some 250 townspeople participated in some way or other, from actors to technicians. The ensemble's final season garnered some $4,000, with profits distributed to Humboldt State College for scholarships, to the Trinidad Potters Guild and to the LaVerne Krei Dance Studio.

Sponsors included the Arcata Community Players, Kate Buchanan, Evelyn Cerini and Mr. and Mrs. Donald Dahlen. Honorary board members were Asta Cullberg, Andrew Genzoli, Monica Hadley, George Hale, Kate Buchanan, William Hover, Jean Neilson, Mary Sample, Jessie Sorenson and John Van Duzer.

Here Pete Haines and Jacque Ames perform in *The Boy Friend*. (Courtesy of the HSU Library, Humboldt County Collection.)

May 10, 1971
Old City Hall Comes Down

THE OLD CITY HALL WAS TORN DOWN BY Johnson Structures. Walls were pulled inward with the help of a crawler tractor and wire cable. About 100,000 board feet of the redwood lumber was salvaged by the firm, and windows and other materials were recycled. What shape was the building in? "They just don't make them like this any more," a spokesman said.

Built in 1896, the building was home of the Masons and Odd Fellows as well as the City but was demolished because there was no money to bring it up to present-day seismic safety standards.

The vacant lot was then turned into a parking lot used by the Hotel Arcata and other area businesses, with flower planters cultivated by community groups. It remained that way until 2005, when a new building was built on the site. (Courtesy of the HSU Library, Humboldt County Collection.)

October 1, 1971
The Train Station Closes

"OK, WE'RE ALL DONE WITH THIS STATION." That's all Station Manager Paul Verville could say as he closed up the Arcata Train Deport for the last time.

Permission to close the Arcata Train Depot of the Northwestern Pacific Railroad was granted by the California Public Utilities Commission. The railroad wanted the station closed, it said, because the type and amount of business handled did not warrant continued maintenance of an agency or a building.

The application to discontinue the agency was first filed March 15 of this year. It would have been granted earlier if the City of Arcata had not opposed the request. At that time, Councilman Ward Falor commented that a city loses some of its stature when it loses its railroad station.

In former days, the station handled passengers, freight, express, and all the other items associated with a railroad. However, at present, Paul Verville, station agent, is the only employee at the station and has been so for the past seven years. (Courtesy of the HSU Library, Humboldt County Collection.)

November 19, 1977
Jacoby's Storehouse Grand Reopening

THE NEWLY RESTORED JACOBY'S STOREHOUSE held its Grand Opening Saturday.

Restoration of the historic landmark, formerly Alexander Brizard's retail store, has been a massive project. The reopened Storehouse features a savings and loan and the Arcata Chamber of Commerce on the first floor, 13 retail stores and an ice-cream parlor on the second floor, Youngberg's restaurant occupying the entire third floor and professional offices on the fourth floor.

Stained and leaded glass windows accent old and new woodwork blended together, with golden oak extensively used throughout the building. Youngberg's fireplace mantel is from Humphrey Bogart's den.

Built in 1857, the original stone building was built by Augustus Jacoby and billed as a "fireproof storehouse." Alexander Brizard bought the building in 1880, and in 1888, he added display windows in the front. In 1907, the building was expanded to the east and south, and two more stories were added.

Brizard's store served Arcata as a full-range emporium until 1969, when the grocery, hardware and furniture departments were closed. In November 1974, the retail operation was closed and plans moved ahead to redevelop the old building on the Plaza. Here Wallace and Samantha Appleton cut the ribbon, as City Councilmember Wes Chesbro looks on. (Courtesy of Bill Chino/CBGT, LLC.)

November 12, 1979
The Plaza Burns

SO CAME THE CALL AT 11 P.M. ON THE NIGHT of Nov. 12, 1979, when fire broke out among a pile of cartons on the loading dock behind the building housing Barnes Rexall Drugs, Deluxe Beauty and Barber Shop and Arthur Johnson's Men's Store. According to the account published in the November 15 *Arcata Union*, "Once ignited, the fire touched off a gas pipe which lit up 'kind of like a blow torch into the attic above.'" So said Chief Bill McKenzie, whose men, though they had arrived only moments after discovery of the blaze, were somewhat hampered in their attempts to quench it due to the construction of the building. The *Union* states, "The attic, shared by all three businesses, was quickly engulfed in flames but protected from firefighters by the roof and ceilings."

"We were on it for an hour before we got it going our way," McKenzie said.

The fire was finally contained at around 2 a.m. through the combined efforts of the Arcata, Eureka and Fairhaven departments. Forty-five paid and volunteer firemen worked on the blaze, and a standby crew watched Tuesday for occasional smoldering spots. The building and its contents were for all intents and purposes completely destroyed at a loss of nearly $450,000.

But the loss could have been even more tragic. All through the history of the department, fire on the Plaza had been the most feared of all the deadly opponents firemen had to face. Inaccessibility and crowding had kept the possibility of a runaway fire utmost in the minds of the firefighters. However, on this occasion as in the past, the speed and skill of the departments involved had prevented further spreading of the fire. While Meyer Bistrin's, the store next to Arthur Johnson's, suffered extensive smoke damage, the building in which it is housed was saved.

The Arcata Police Department (APD) listed the cause of the blaze as "arson under investigation" and again, though attempts to track down the perpetrator were extensive, no clues surfaced. (Courtesy of Dave White/ Arcata Volunteer Fire Department.)

JOHNSON'S
ONLY

April 17, 1983
An Icon Is Born

YOU'VE SEEN HER ON THE PLAZA, AT CO-OP or Humboldt State University (HSU), the flower of Humboldt womanhood, festooned with any number of countercultural cues, calculatedly proletarian garb, buttons espousing causes sweet and snarky, a sage smudge or patchouli aroma and a faraway look in her eye.

Nowhere is the stereotype more completely expressed than in the legendary "Are You a Humboldt Honey?" poster that most everyone has owned and lost sometime during house moves.

The poster depicts what must surely be the mother of all Honeys, bedecked, maybe *laden* is a better term, with every possible hipster accessory, aglow with cool confidence and fully armed to do battle with the dominant paradigm.

For Humboldt Honey poster creator Ingrid Hart (then Ingrid da Silva), the poster that began as a lark has become something of a life changer. Hart, then a 21-year-old Humboldt State University journalism student, had noticed the then-popular "Are You a Valley Girl?" and "Are You a Nerd?" posters and decided that Humboldt's homegrown stereotype was suitable for the same treatment.

The larval Honey was Leoni Nicol. Hart enlisted the services of up-and-coming local photographer Patrick Cudahy. With desktop publishing still a few years off, Hart hired a graphics house to do the typesetting and had the posters printed in Santa Rosa. Her first press run wrought 1,000 copies.

A flood of letters to the editors of local newspapers ensued, decrying the presumed celebration of slovenliness, drug-taking, rebellion and general hippiehood.

Some people, including young men, got it, though.

"Oh, 'Humboldt Honey,' no matter who or what your opponents might be, know you have a very grateful and appreciative proponent in me," wrote Michael R. Langdon of Eureka. "I think I am in love." (Courtesy of Ingrid Hart.)

ARE YOU A HUMBOLDT HONEY?

March 30, 1995
Arcata's Road Warrior

MIGHTY BUT MISUNDERSTOOD, ARCATA'S Tymco 600 Regenerative Air Street Sweeper is a one-vehicle mechanized division, roaming the City's byways daily in a never-ending battle to clear them of dross and debris.

The mass of pumps, blowers, sprinklers and rotating brushes begins its rounds at 6 a.m., circling the town in loose, counterclockwise loops.

Driver Gary Page starts his rounds sitting on the left-hand side of the cockpit, then switches over to the other set of controls on the right-hand side of the cabin to cleanse the other side of the street.

In the twilight, the street sweeper's red blinkers and amber rear flashers create strobing reflections in buildings that it passes. Dogs are roused to bark at the marauding machine, while sensible house cats simply seek cover.

Page is unapologetic for causing the pets to cower and run for the bushes with the street sweeper's early morning symphony of swirling brushes and flashing lights. "What are you gonna do?" he asks. "You gotta have the noise to suck up all the material."

Here the street sweeper makes a ghostly pass through the Plaza, inhaling effluvium from the previous evening's festivities. (Photographs by Kevin L. Hoover/Arcata Eye.)

November 19, 1996
The Pack-Out

FOR MONTHS THE TRAVELERS AND THEIR animal companions had made a home in the redwood stump in a little-traveled area off Trail No. 1 in the Arcata Community Forest. Discovered and shooed away, it was up to others to pack out the elaborate shelter and piles of garbage.

Enter the Backcountry Horsemen of America. For them and their mules, the garbage detail was business as usual. Last year, the horsemen hauled some 3,000 pounds of waste and debris out of remote trail camps in the Trinity Alps and Marble Mountains.

Arriving at the Community Forest campsite, City of Arcata workers dismantled the forest hidey-holes, cobbled together from boxes, supermarket bread trays, tree branches and other debris, and stuffed with old clothing and cooking implements, including a barbecue.

Horsemen Dick Wild and Tom Acord "mantee pack" their mule team partners, Pauline (seen here) and Molly Tamale, with camp materials. "They're incredibly smart," said Wild. "And strong, too. She could swing me around like a rag doll," he said of the 1,200-pound Molly. Pauline weighs in at a petite 950 pounds.

By day's end, some 800 pounds of garbage had been trundled back to a truck on the main trail for disposal at the City Corp Yard. (Photograph by Kevin L. Hoover/ Arcata Eye.)

July 17, 1997
Pete the Ragman Saves a Life

Pete Villarreal, known to Arcatans as Raggedy Pete or Pete the Ragman, sprang into action Thursday morning at 11 a.m. to save a damsel in serious distress.

Identified only as Cathy, the woman had collapsed near the Intermodal Transit Facility. "She fell down," said Pete, who cushioned her fall, then went for help. "She said, 'I feel like I'm going to die,' so I ran as fast as I can for the Fire Department."

Firefighters at the Ninth Street fire station summoned police and paramedics to the scene, and the 46-year-old woman was rushed to Mad River Community Hospital.

"She was comatose and cyanotic behind some bushes," said APD Lt. Randy Mendosa. "If she'd been there much longer, she probably would have died." He congratulated Pete for his alertness and decisive action.

"I love people with my open heart," Pete said.

An Arcata institution, Pete was a fixture on the streets for a quarter century until his departure for Hermiston, Ore., in January 2008. Hillary and Daniel McAlarney are seen here with Pete. (Photograph by Terrence McNally/Arcata Eye.)

July 19, 1997
Green Party Convention, Reaction

WITH A GREEN PARTY ON THE ARCATA CITY Council, the California Greens held their annual convention at the Veterans' Memorial Building.

About 100 representatives attended a City Council meeting, toured various Humboldt County sites, held workshops and socialized. "Arcata has any number of things we're proud to show visitors from around the state," said Melanie Williams, chair of the Humboldt Greens.

Santa Monica City Councilmember Michael Feinstein said the party would remain true to its basic principles by "practicing the duality of being inside and outside the system," and be continually self-renewing. "We intend to always return to the base of social justice," he said.

The Vets' Hall is across the street from Arcata traditionalists Lois and Robin Arkley, who, along with 15 to 20 others, participated in an anti-Green counterdemonstration by picketing outside the building for a half hour or so.

"They're socialists, with a planned economy," said Robin. He said members of the group had "trivialized" ideological opponents.

Lois objected to the Greens' "intellectual annexation" of issues such as the environment, noting that the Arcata Community Forest was established without leftist political assistance. "In Arcata, we see no smoking on the Plaza and we're heading toward no cars on the Plaza. Seems like more government, doesn't it?" she asked. (Photograph by Kevin L. Hoover/ Arcata Eye.)

March 2, 1999
The Greening of G Street

MEMBERS OF ARCATA MAINSTREET, LED BY Executive Director Michael Behney, gathered early Saturday morning to plant seven new Akebono flowering cherry trees along G Street on the Plaza. The trees are known for their wide canopy and soft pink flowers.

The street trees were Behney's brainchild and, like most everything in Arcata, weren't installed without controversy. Some questioned the wisdom of adding anything that blocks the relatively rare Humboldt sunlight, while one resident feared that the trees could turn into torches from discarded cigarette butts, then set buildings alight.

But the trees themselves have been proven vulnerable to the drunken depredations of late-night taverngoers, who sometimes use the trees to steady themselves, exceeding their structural capacities.

Nonetheless, Mainstreet and the City hope to eventually encircle the Plaza with street trees, greening the downtown.

Pitching in to plant the trees are, left to right, Alex Stillman, Paul Rex, Jason Wright, Michael Behney, Ann Russell, Connie Stewart and Mary Gearheart. (Photograph by Kevin L. Hoover/Arcata Eye.)

April 25, 1999
Time for Arcata

HAVING PIONEERED THE FIRST MEDICAL marijuana licensing system, Arcata earned the interest of national newsmagazine *Time*. For a story titled, "Here's My Marijuana Card, Officer," the magazine organized a photo shoot on the Plaza featuring Chief of Police Mel Brown, plus medical cannabis advocates and patients.

Wrote *Time*, "It is not that Mel Brown, police chief of this tie-dye-and-tofu town, set out to flout federal law. But here he is, a 53-year-old father of two who has never inhaled, issuing laminated and embossed get-out-of-jail-free cards for partakers of the infamous Humboldt bud, a potent local variety of marijuana. 'You can photograph me,' he tells a reporter genially, 'but not reclining on a bearskin rug and smoking a joint.'"

Time noted that Arcata "lies in the heart of the Emerald Triangle, the three lush California counties of Humboldt, Mendocino and Trinity, 275 miles north of San Francisco as the spotted owl flies."

The story outlined Arcata's Prop 215 implementation system as a bid for pragmatism: "... Chief Brown considers his policy one of common sense. 'Out of self-preservation,' he says, he set up his own system. Now about 100 local residents have sat for mug shots, agreed to let Brown talk to their physicians, and walked away with a 'City of Arcata Proposition 215 Identification Card.' Flash it as you are toking up and you won't be arrested, unless you've got more than 10 marijuana plants a limit imposed to distinguish users from illegal dealers." (Photograph by Kevin L. Hoover/Arcata Eye.)

November 26, 1999

Cab 10's Journey Ends

ARCATA CAB DRIVER, RANCHER, SECURITY GUARD, newspaper columnist and author Randy Collenberg, 47, died early Friday morning, November 26, in a rollover vehicle accident on State Route 44, about four and a half miles west of Susanville in Lassen County. Also killed were Collenberg's wife, Dannette, 31, and the family's babysitter, Janice Bradbury, 57. Hospitalized with moderate to minor injuries were Collenberg's sons, David, 18, Zachary, 10, and Benjamin, 5.

The family had been traveling to Reno, Nev., for a Thanksgiving holiday with the children's godparents.

According to a California Highway Patrol Report, their eastbound Chevy Astro van hit a patch of frosty roadway while negotiating a curve. Bradbury, who was driving, apparently lost control of the vehicle, which was not equipped with snow tires or chains.

Randy Collenberg was well known to readers of local newspapers as the West Coast Cabbie. His colorful, true-life tales of life as a taxi driver were closely followed and extremely popular among many segments of the community, from the seniors he drove to and from Adult Day Care at Mad River Community Hospital to Humboldt State University students who used his transportation services after visits to downtown bars.

Collenberg's many passengers and readers expressed extreme shock at the loss of such a dynamic, larger-than-life figure with so much going for him. The gregarious taxi driver was on a first-name basis with much of the population of northern Humboldt.

Arcata Police Chief Mel Brown remembered Collenberg as "a real people person." Said Brown, "I never saw him in a bad mood or having a down day. Every time you saw that yellow cab and before you saw the '10' on it, you saw the wave."

Yellow Cab Company of Eureka plans to retire the Number 10. Here, Randy is beside his famous "Luxurious Yellow Cruiser." (Courtesy of Randy Collenberg.)

Yellow
Yello
Cab
Co.
442-4

December 15, 1999
Arcata's Lake of Poison

FOR DECADES, THE LOUISIANA-PACIFIC Corporation (L-P) pumped manufacturing wastes, formaldehyde-laced tannins and lignins, straight into a 22-acre log pond behind the West End Road factory. First discovered by Fish and Game Warden Jon Wilcox, the pond contains an estimated 89,000 cubic yards of toxic sludge.

On Dec. 15, 1999, Humboldt County sued L-P, alleging 422 counts of violating state air and water pollution and wildlife protection laws. Theoretically, fines could have topped $80 million.

The matter was swiftly resolved. In February 2000, District Attorney Terry Farmer announced a settlement in which L-P would pay the equivalent of $712,500. The company got a $250,000 credit for equipment modifications. Remaining monies went to various agencies and the City of Arcata.

The black sludge was not removed and remains at the site as an overgrown expanse of toxic waste. Environmental services director Mark Andre said the material is "stable and localized as far as we (City staff) know." Nor is it being added to.

If the lawn area of Arcata's downtown Plaza had perimeter walls 18.25 feet in height, the toxic sludge in the former L-P log pond on West End Road would fill it to the top.

Sold to Hambro Forest Products in 2003, the factory is now known as Humboldt Flakeboard. The employee-owned company has initiated environmentally friendly practices, including advanced biological remediation of its toxic emissions. (Courtesy of Jon Wilcox/California Department of Fish and Game.)

February 22, 2000
Sandy's Sanctuary Spared

THE FIELD WEST OF SANDY GIUNTOLI'S HOUSE had been fallow for decades following the closure of the California Barrel factory in the 1960s. From the kitchen window they've looked out since 1936, Sandy and wife May enjoyed seeing birds splash in the pond.

When a pile of old blacktop chunks was dumped on an abandoned railroad spur there in the 1980s, Giuntoli, now 82, swung into action. "It looked bad, so I leveled it off and started planting."

The result is a plush bird feeding sanctuary, a riotous mix of plants Giuntoli believes are of comfort to winged passersby, including wild onions, calla lilies, nasturtiums and hollyhock.

The charm of Giuntoli's installation wasn't lost on Tom Perrett, whose new Tomas Jewelry factory has risen up beside it. Sandy's sanctuary actually rests partly on Perrett's property, and as the new manufacturing facility went up, construction workers wanted to tear out the bird playground to ease access by heavy equipment.

"We had the subcontractors going crazy," Perrett said. "They were encouraging us to take it down."

But it was not to be. "We really worked around it," Perrett said. "It did affect our plans a little bit."

Its fate secure, Giuntoli has since dressed up the sanctuary further, adding a rock border. "A lot of people like it," he said. "They come by and say, 'I hope they don't take that out.'"

One recent afternoon, Giuntoli was seen planting still more flowers across the street next to a culvert pipe.

"I thought this would make it look a little nicer," he said, patting down some freshly turned earth. (Photograph by Kevin L. Hoover/Arcata Eye.)

June 24, 2000

Arcata Bowl

Game Over

AFTER 43 YEARS, ARCATA BOWL'S PINSETTING gear fell silent for the last time last Saturday night, June 24 after attempts to receive a 10-year lease on the building failed. In 1998, the bowling alley considered closure after a $1,000-a-month rent increase and passage of legal restrictions on smoking in such establishments.

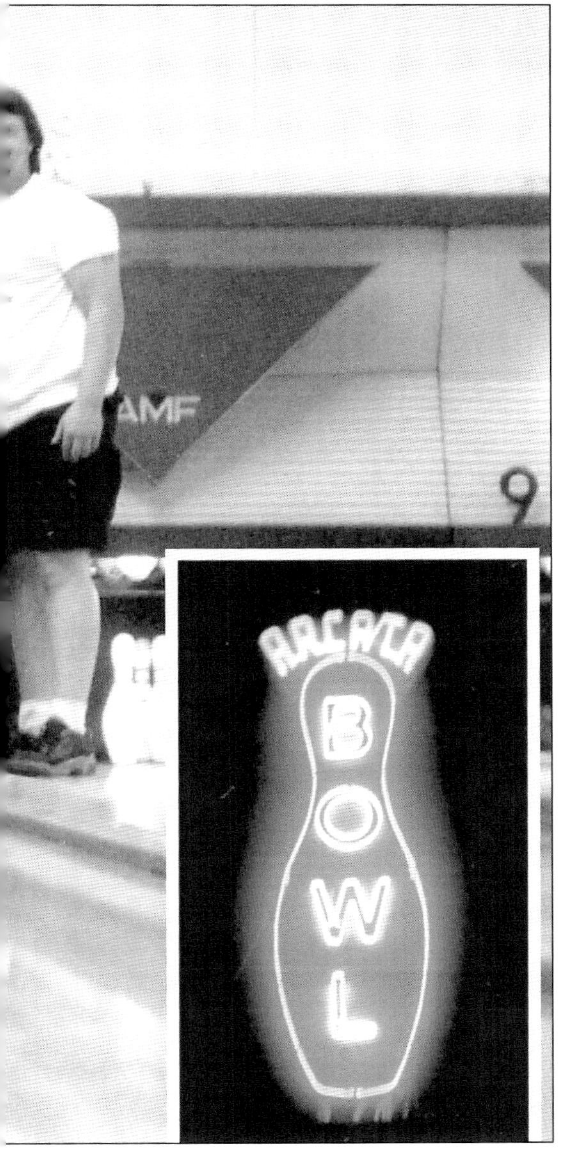

Arcata also lost the Pin Room, an accessible venue for fledgling musical talent and a last bastion of indoor smoking.

All involved expressed bittersweet emotions. "It's really a crying shame," said Kent Ames, the alley's pin jockey. "This is a sad day for me."

"This place is my social life," said bowler Paige Tomaselli. "I got so attached."

"I'm pretty bummed this place is closing," said bowler Rodney Ferrario. (Photograph by Kevin L. Hoover/Arcata Eye.)

January 31, 2001
Arcata's Living Room

RESISTANCE TO NEW LAWS AIMED AT MAKING Arcata's business areas more visitor-friendly is escalating, and Wednesday night's council meeting saw speakers, political organizers and even a street theater troupe venting protest.

The meeting's tone was forecast outside the entrance of City Hall, where a couch and TV set were used as props in an impromptu skit called "The Plaza: Arcata's Livingroom."

"Does anybody want to buy anything?" one of the actresses repeatedly blurted, a reference to charges that the City's goal is to gentrify business areas. A performer nominally dressed as a dog hopped about the pseudo–living room, while another thespian, apparently depicting the plight of disenfranchised sidewalk sitters, wandered aimlessly around the small entryway, occasionally declaring, "It sucks!"

But despite high-visibility opposition and at-times strident protest during public comment at the last two meetings, the council isn't buying arguments that the new laws contradict the will of the community.

Passed at the January 3 meeting, the ordinances restrict cigarette smoking on an expanded Plaza, while stationary dogs and sidewalk blocking is prohibited in commercial areas ranging from the Plaza through Northtown. They're tailored, say backers, to making central Arcata more widely accessible.

Mayor Connie Stewart tried to calm fears that police would leverage the ordinances to clear "Arcata's beloved lower class citizens," as read one sign hoisted at a previous meeting, so that monied folk could have the Plaza to themselves. She cautioned curmudgeons watching at home that the new laws would not sweep the streets clean of hippies when they become law February 2. (Photograph by Kevin L. Hoover/Arcata Eye.)

July 25, 2001
The Fire of 2001

On July 25, 2001, sometime after the close of business, a fire somehow began in the attic of the Northcoast Environmental Center (NEC) on Ninth Street. The fire was not reported until 11:22 p.m., by which time it was well underway and had spread to the adjoining Marino's tavern, an 1880s-vintage building with no fire prevention measures built in.

Some 11 fire engines and 65 firefighters from Arcata and neighboring towns responded as the fire, fueled by the NEC's extensive library, spread to the Arcata Paint building. The blaze was battled through the night as firefighters tried to keep it from spreading to the Feuerwerker Building across the street. That building had been rebuilt after its predecessor burned down on New Year's Eve 1995.

The next morning, firefighters doused embers as NEC employees picked through the ruins to salvage what they could. Though the NEC's 30-year collection of archives was lost, miraculously, several computers and filing cabinets survived. Data from the scorched computers' hard drives was transferred, aiding recovery. Arcata swang into action, too, with businesses and citizens donating resources to rebuild the NEC. (Photograph by Kevin L. Hoover/Arcata Eye.)

AFD

February 24, 2003
The Passing of Orick Johnny

KNOWN AS "ORICK JOHNNY," THE GRUFF, ELFIN figure was often seen thumbing a ride between Arcata and his boyhood home of Orick. Volunteer chauffeurs were often rewarded with Johnny stubbing out his trademark Lucky Strike on the car's seat. "When you pick up John, you don't expect burgeoning gratitude," said Genaro Calabrese.

His trademark waddle stemmed from a childhood whittling accident with a double-handled draw knife, which severed the tendons in his knee. With limited medical care in backwoods Orick in 1931, the accident imparted Johnny an exaggerated saunter for the rest of his life.

An inveterate reader, Johnny took in several newspapers each day, sometimes enjoying a packaged lemon pie washed down with a half pint of half-and-half and followed by an unfiltered cigarette.

Conversation often centered on the evils of politicians, "hippies" and Humboldt State University, which he held responsible for Arcata's decline, as he saw it. Johnny preferred Arcata's boomtown decades as a center for timber and fishing. "The college ruined Arcata," he once said.

"Johnny was a mild and simple man you couldn't help loving," said former City Councilmember Robert Noble. "He touched my life." Here Johnny waits for his ride in a chair provided him by bank employees at Jacoby's Storehouse. (Photograph by Kevin L. Hoover/Arcata Eye.)

March 8, 2003
Old St. Mary's Church Goes Up in Flames

ONE HUNDRED NINETEEN YEARS OF ARCATA history—and a chapter yet unwritten—fell to ashes Saturday morning as St. Mary's Church on 16th Street burned to the ground.

The Arcata Volunteer Fire Department was called to the scene at 5:12 a.m., arriving to find the historic wooden structure fully involved in flame. Thirty-seven firefighters, including many from neighboring communities, had the blaze quelled after an hour and a half.

Subsequent investigation indicated that a traveler's campfire in the building's crawl space was responsible for the fire. Church officials had pointed out camp debris to visiting reporters two days prior to the fire. Access had been ineffectually blocked by nailed boards, though intruders routinely broke in through back and side doors.

The pre-fire media tour had been organized to help build interest in a church restoration drive that was just getting underway.

St. Mary's Church had been built for $2,000 in 1884 and was closed in 1984. (Photograph by Terrence McNally/Arcata Eye.)

AT 1690 JANES ROAD

June 23, 2003
A Thumb Well Done

The thumb was stolen by night from the statue of President William McKinley on the Plaza sometime in May 2003. Noticed days later, the thumb's disappearance mobilized Arcata. Mayor Bob Ornelas personally posted a $500 reward for its return. Area sculptors pondered possibilities for crafting a replacement thumb.

The case was cracked when a stranger asked Billy Dobbins for a cigarette at Clam Beach. As he rolled one, the man handed him a pudgy bronze appendage. "I thought it was a toe," Dobbins said. "It's off the statue of McKinley," the man told him.

Dobbins, an unemployed general laborer from Abilene, Texas, was aware of the $500 reward and notified authorities. The thumb thief was granted immunity in exchange for the thumb. It was returned June 13, 2003.

Concluding a story that made national news, welder Mike Callaghan reattached Big Bill's missing rigid digit, then patina-matched it with an acid treatment.

Four days after accepting his reward in a City Hall ceremony, Dobbins was arrested after what police said was a drunken brawl at a McKinleyville trailer park. Dobbins was found passed out in his car not far from where he had first seen the stolen thumb. He claimed he'd been surrounded by pro-thumb theft vigilantes who called him a "snitch."

"There was four of them and one of me," Dobbins said. "They lied and said I threw something at their car."

Meanwhile, Mayor Ornelas used the returned thumb to poke the Bush Administration in the eye. "They couldn't find bin Laden; they couldn't find Saddam Hussein; they couldn't find weapons of mass destruction," the mayor said. "We found McKinley's thumb." (Photograph by Terrence McNally/Arcata Eye.)

August 30, 2004
Traffic School on Old Arcata Road

THE FIRST DAY OF FALL CLASSES AT BAYSIDE'S Jacoby Creek School brought new and returning students, traffic and picketers.

Concerns about traffic and chronic speeding on the narrow straightaway drew neighbors to the streets with signs in hand. Many used the occasion to protest plans for a large new development at the former Roger's Garage complex, a plan that was later cancelled. "Big Development = Big Traffic Jam," read one sign. "My Dad Bikes Here," read another.

The traffic-hammered Old Arcata Road section later gained a number of traffic-calming features developed by the all-citizen Transportation Safety Committee and engineered by the City's Public Works department. These include no less than five speed humps, bike lanes and sidewalks.

Arcata has aggressively sought to calm traffic and make the City more bicycle- and pedestrian-friendly. High-use intersections have seen installation of roundabouts and smaller neighborhood traffic circles, speed tables and pedestrian-refuge islands. (Photograph by Kevin L. Hoover/Arcata Eye.)

It's About
SAFETY
Development
=
TRAFFIC
NIGHTMARE!

December 31, 2004
Dopey New Year

NEW YEAR'S EVE MORNING DAWNED WITH A carpet of green on a section of sidewalk in the 900 block of F Street. There an unknown marijuana grower discarded unprofitable harvest residue, low-THC leaf and stem material, in a 30-foot swath of green.

A witness said the grower was laughing as he blazed the trail of trimmings, estimated at 20 pounds.

A number of individuals waiting for services at the nearby Arcata Endeavor/Intermodal Transit Facility soon descended on the swath of green, plucking overlooked nuggets from the sidewalk. "It was a footrace," said a witness.

One fast-working gleaner wasn't terribly selective, making off with a garbage bag full of material hastily swept off the sidewalk. That may be why, later that day, a woman downtown complained of purchasing marijuana with pine needles in it.

Ranger Bob Murphy was called to the scene and scooped up the dopey delivery. He said local stoners told him they planned to cook with the feeble weed so as to concentrate its potency. (Photograph by Kevin L. Hoover/ Arcata Eye.)

STOP
2PTZ661

May 27, 2006
Extreme Makeover

SCULPTOR/ARTIST/MUSICIAN DUANE FLATMO'S daring designs are always a crowd favorite during the annual Great Arcata-to-Ferndale World Championship Kinetic Sculpture Race, the nation's original human-powered art competition.

The race began in 1969 on Main Street in Ferndale. Legend has it that Glorious Founder Hobart Brown had built a kinetic contraption and planned a ride, when a fellow artist challenged him to a race.

The first marathon race was held in 1974. Just three entries braved the Field's Landing-to-Eureka course. The winner that year was Danny Sizemore's "Watergate Streaker." Since then, the race has grown in length and in size, with dozens of highly sophisticated entries launching from the Plaza with the blasting of the noon siren every Memorial Day weekend Saturday.

Hobart Brown passed away Nov. 7, 2007, but his spirit lives on the Kinetic Sculpture Race.

Here Flatmo and his dedicated crew move "Extreme Makeover" down Eighth Street toward the Arcata Bottom on May 27, 2006. (Photograph by Kevin L. Hoover/Arcata Eye.)

EXTREME
MAKEOVER
PIERSON
BUILDING CENTER

November 15, 2006
Arcata's Artisan Tradition

ARCATA ESTABLISHED ITSELF EARLY ON AS A hub for artisan manufacturers. From early tradesmen fashioning work necessities to today's creators of high-end art, that tradition of craftsmanship continues.

George Bucquet, left, of Mad River Glass, whose work is distributed at galleries throughout the country, prepares a commissioned bowl in 2006 with the help of John Sarver. Bucquet creates contemporary, hand-formed cast glass imagery both meditative and visually stimulating. With precision timing, Bucquet and his assistants pour hot glass, thick and translucent as honey, into a handmade sand mold, then press it into shape in Mad River Glass's studio in a converted television station on 16th Street. A mold is individually created for each casting, and the colored molten glass, formulated from scratch, is melted to 2350 F in a custom furnace. After several days of cooling in an annealing oven, each bowl is hand detailed with copper, silver and gold leaf.

Bucquet's work is found in galleries around the world and in the private collections of Rupert Murdoch, Bill Gates, Irvin Borowsky, Noel and Janene Hilliard, and the Estate of Jerry Garcia. His work can also be found in the permanent collections of the U.S. Embassy, Ottawa, Canada, the Musée des Arts Décoratifs, Lausanne, Switzerland, the Asheville Museum of Art, N.C., the National Liberty Museum, Philadelphia, Pa., and the White House. (Photograph by Terrence McNally/Arcata Eye.)

January 1, 2007
Happy New Year!

ARCATA USHERED IN 2007 WITH A ROILING riot of music, dancing, smooching and statue-climbing, as celebrants jammed the Plaza in what has become an annual New Year's Eve affair. Apart from a couple of fist fights and some flower trampling (and more than a few hangovers), no casualties were reported.

Arcata's Public Works Department was probably glad to say goodbye to 2006, since that year recorded the second-highest bill for vandalism ever—more than $29,000 in graffiti, trashed campsites, donutted park turf, destroyed trees and playground equipment and even severe retribution unleashed against various downspouts.

None of which mattered very much across town at Mad River Community Hospital, where Arcata's first babies of 2007 were busy coming into the world. Baby Tess was born to Nancy and Phil Taylor (and big sister Lila) at 10:50 p.m. December 31, while baby Raven was born to Kerrie and Gary Brown at 12:04 a.m. Jan. 1, 2007. (Photograph by Terrence McNally/Arcata Eye.)

January 5, 2007
Hunt Barn Burns

THE ARCATA BOTTOM CONTINUES TO BE USED for agriculture and livestock production, with numerous historic structures signifying the tradition. Gradually, though, the tests of time tend to return the area to its original marshy condition.

One was the Hunt Barn, unused for years after its surrounding lands were merged into the Arcata Marsh and Wildlife Sanctuary wetlands complex.

While historians, preservationists and City of Arcata officials considered restoration, illegal campers used the barn for socializing and shelter, filling it with litter. Walls were stripped for wood to fuel campfires, which burned portions of the building, and powder post beetles infested beams. All the while, wind and weather took its toll, blowing down walls and putting holes in the roof.

The Arcata Fire Protection District advocated demolition, but that recommendation was countered with talk of marshaling a volunteer corps of interested building contractors to refurbish the structure.

Finally, a fire of unknown origin ended the debate, leveling the sagging Hunt Barn on Jan. 5, 2007, and eliminating a once-noble working structure that had become a safety and fire hazard. (Photograph by Terrence McNally/Arcata Eye.)

July 4, 2007
Jubilation at the Jubilee

ARCATA'S FOURTH OF JULY JUBILEE ALMOST lost its patriotic display when the Chamber of Commerce couldn't locate donors to fund the annual fireworks, which follow the traditional Plaza jubilee and Humboldt Crabs game. The matter became public following publication of a June 5 *Arcata Eye* story, unleashing an explosion of consternation.

Driven by patriotism and tradition, Lane DeVries, a naturalized citizen who immigrated to the United States in 1983, offered to pay the $10,000 fireworks fee himself. "I'm proud to be an American, and fireworks are an integral part of American history," he said. Arcata's history, too. "It's the heartbeat of our town," he said. "What is the Arcata Fourth of July without fireworks?"

DeVries called former Mayor Carl Pellatz, who contacted Fireworks by Boom Boom in Hayfork. It turned out that Boom Boom, which has put on shows for Eureka, Crescent City, McKinleyville High School, Sears Point Raceway and Walt Disney World, among other customers, has coveted the Arcata gig for some time, but another company—since booked up—had a lock on it.

Second on a list of "Guiding Principles" posted on the wall of DeVries's Sun Valley Floral Farms office is "Dedicated to being a good neighbor and improving the community in which we live."

"It's just not right to not have fireworks in Arcata," DeVries said, shaking his head. "That notion there, I just couldn't stand it." Pellatz said he and DeVries were only being responsible community members. "It's just the typical Arcata people that want to make sure things get done," he said.

With a lot of help from its friends, Arcata's 2007 Fourth of July Jubilee was complete, including a starred and striped Michelle Dobosh, left, and Angeline Wolski, right, escorted by Mr. McKinley on the Plaza that sunny day. (Photograph by Terrence McNally/ Arcata Eye.)

July 13, 2007
Mules of Brizard/Jacoby's

AS AN EARLY NORTHERN CALIFORNIA SUPPLY point, Arcata's mid-19th-century prominence was built on the backs of mules.

The Union Company had established the town of Union (later renamed Arcata) as a port linking to inland gold mines. Prior to Union's establishment, miners had to travel to Sacramento for supplies, but once founded, pack trains brought supplies from the coast to mines on the Klamath, Trinity and Salmon rivers.

Mules brought up on the Sonoma Trail fetched $300 or more, and pack trains commonly used 10 to 55 of the burly beasts, some as many as 75 to 100. Trains of that size were operated by Alexander Brizard, Thomas Bair, William Lod and Isaac Minor.

The animals were used for mail delivery in some parts of the county until 1915.

On July 13, 2007, a 21st-century traveling team happened to stop in front of Jacoby's Storehouse, formerly Brizard Store, for a rest, paying inadvertent homage to innumerable forebears. (Photograph by Terrence McNally/ Arcata Eye.)

July 17, 2007
Bivalves by the Bay

THE ANNUAL ARCATA BAY OYSTER FESTIVAL continues to draw bivalve enthusiasts every June, in a daylong celebration with oyster calling, music and fun for the whole family.

Humboldt Bay, with Arcata on its northern shore, is one of the most pristine and biologically important estuaries on the West Coast, hosting a diverse array of species. Among them are 141 invertebrate, 110 fish, 251 bird and 30 mammal species. The Bay is a critical link for migrating and wintering waterbirds in the chain of coastal wetlands from the Arctic Circle to South America. It annually supports millions of waterbirds, shorebirds, raptors and songbirds.

Humboldt Bay also supplies some two-thirds of the oysters harvested for human consumption in California.

Here Shaye Harty, left, and Gina Figueroa, right, compete in the June Oyster Calling Contest. (Photograph by Terrence McNally/ Arcata Eye.)

The Alibi

July 24, 2007
Ranger Bob Retires

HE CLEANED UP THE CAMPS IN THE COMMUNITY Forest, made peace in Redwood Park, worked wonders at the Marsh and Wildlife Sanctuary and reduced abuse on the Plaza. Now, Arcata Police Park Ranger Bob Murphy has one last task, which he'll take care of this Friday, and that's hanging up his hat. After 25 years, Ranger Bob is retiring from APD.

For his firm-but-gentle enforcement, Murphy earns plaudits from street urchins and superiors alike. "I think he's fair," said a young man in an orange Phoenix Suns jersey as he shared a doobie with friends at Ninth and H streets Sunday night. "Not lenient, but fair. He took my weed one time and said, 'Get the hell on outta here.'"

"He's gained the respect of most of his 'clients,'" said Police Chief Randy Mendosa. "He speaks their language."

Among Ranger Bob's duties has been enforcing Title IV, Chapter 3, Section 4305 of the Arcata Municipal Code, which states, "The City further finds that noises which are boisterous, penetrating, repetitive, of unusual rhythmic or tonal character, of long duration, or that are unreasonably distracting in any other manner, are especially likely to be detrimental and harmful to the Downtown Plaza area and offensive to the area's residents, merchants, employees, patrons and other users of ordinary sensitivity." That puts the Plaza's bongo pilots in Murphy's sights, but he usually allowed them to thump away until someone complained, then cordially encouraged them to pound the skins elsewhere.

Murphy takes most solace from Redwood Park's before-and-after upgrade. "The kids would be here," he said amid gleeful children at summer day camp, "and my guys would be over there washing their feet." Now, Murphy said, "I come up to the park and see kids play, people playing frisbee, the butterflies butterflying." (Photograph by Kevin L. Hoover/Arcata Eye.)

July 28, 2007
Take Me Out to a Crabs Game

THE HUMBOLDT CRABS ARE THE NATION'S oldest semipro baseball team and draw all types of fans. Here the Humboldt Crab Grass Band members perform the ragtag ensemble's "Chicken Dance" during a July 2007 seventh-inning stretch.

More than just a ball game, the summertime Crabs baseball days at the Arcata Ball Park are a cultural multimedia event. Along with baseball, beer, tofu dogs and even peanuts, fans enjoy the musical strains of the Crab Grass Band, which might favor the crowd with songs by Aerosmith, Iron Butterfly and the Beatles.

The band, which formed in 1983, is comprised of members and alumni of the equally iconoclastic HSU Marching Lumberjacks band, plus ad hoc additions. (Photograph by Terrence McNally/Arcata Eye.)

October 12, 2007
The BSS Building Begins

WITH A CROWD OF MORE THAN 200 GUESTS present, Humboldt State University's new Behavioral and Social Sciences (BSS) Building was dedicated in a ceremony Friday, October 12. The ceremony was held in the courtyard between the two BSS structures. The HSU Calypso Band opened and closed the festivities. President Rollin C. Richmond presided.

"The dedication today of the Behavioral and Social Sciences Building, which includes facilities for Native American people that were specially designed with their values in mind, is a sign of the overall momentum at HSU," Richmond said.

The $30 million Behavioral and Social Sciences Building is an 84,000-square-foot replacement building that is the new home to 10 departments, including the Center for Indian Community Development, Native American Studies, Languages and Cultures, Social Work, Philosophy and Religious Studies. The building features lecture rooms, research space, facility and graduate offices, gallery space, academic computing labs and a psychology clinic.

Standing five stories high, the Behavioral and Social Sciences Building is not just the tallest building on campus, it is also the greenest. The BSS meets the LEED Gold rating and is currently the most environmentally friendly and sustainable building in the California State University system.

The final BSS design is much different than the building originally proposed in the early 1990s. That design bore few environmental features, faced away from the sun and was located on narrow Union Street to the west, placing residential homes, many occupied by HSU alumni, in its shadows. Though the university prevailed in a lawsuit brought by the City of Arcata to force better environmental compliance, President Richmond nonetheless ordered a revision and relocation of the BSS Building to increase its eco-friendliness, energy efficiency and minimize its impacts on the surrounding community.

Here former HSU President Alistair McCrone, left, and President Richmond cut the ribbon for the BSS Building. (Photograph by Terrence McNally/Arcata Eye.)